Hacking

I0011386

Beginner's Ultimate Expert Guide

By Marvin Hobbs

Table of Contents

Introduction

Hello and thank you for buying this book. If you are wanting to learn all the basics of hacking, you have come to the right place. This book will have all the information you need to practice basic hacking skills. In this book you will find information on the history of hacking, how to hack, what systems are best to start out on, and why you would need to know how to hack. Remember, this book is for informational purposes only, and is not to be used for any illicit activity. All in affiliation with this book do not take responsibility for any illegal activities based upon the writing in these pages. Thank you and enjoy!

Chapter 1: History of Hacking

Hacking didn't start at the beginning of the internet era. In fact it began way before internet was a widespread household necessity. Before internet really existed. As long as there have been electronic devices, people have been fiddling with them, trying to find shortcuts in their processors. Hacking, while becoming wildly popular as of late, is not a new concept.

Hacking is more of a way a life, than a type of hobby. Hacking is altering the flow of communication on anything. You can even have hacks in life. Hacking makes life and everyday things a lot easier, and sometimes, though it can be illegal, it is often necessary. Follow along this chapter to learn some very interesting things about the history of hacking, and what hacking is exactly.

What is Hacking?

Hacking is the interruption and manipulation of normal network connections and normal network activity. This is done by a hacker through scripts or network programming. Those will be talked about later on in the book. The term hacking refers to activities of only good intentions, but is often confused with cracking, or breaking into mainframe systems with bad intentions. However, as of late, any form of computer espionage or sabotage. Hacking is the use of worms to break into a systems firewall to gain more information about the systems inner workings, and allows people to see if there is any problems with the software itself.

A beginning hacker can get pre-packaged scripts to assist in hacking from pretty much anywhere off the internet, but be careful, you don't want to download them from just anywhere, because you will soon learn that downloads are the easiest way to install a virus that allows someone to steal your personal information.

Hacker used to be associated with only good things, as hacker used to only mean someone skilled in computer code and programming. These people would fix bugs in a computer system, and remedy unsatisfactory processors. However, some of these good guys got good at breaking into password protected files, and began cracking encrypted and private files.

Hackers use various tools to break into these files to do their cracking. These tools can cause major damage to someone who doesn't have anti-virus installed on their computer. These tools, such as viruses, bugs, worms, glitches and vulnerabilities, make for a nasty problem to whoever receives them.

History of Hacking

Hacking first came around in the 1870s when some teenagers were thrown off the new phone systems due to figuring out how to make free calls. Since then it has expanded and officially been named hacking.

Hacking didn't start becoming a big thing until a hundred years later when MIT had students work on their giant main frame computers, and use their skills to fix problems by writing codes that manipulated data going into the main frame of the systems.

In 1970, a man by the name of John Draper was arrested multiple times for manipulating the phone lines to make long distance calls without having to pay. He discovered that if you blow a certain tone into the phone receiver, it instructed the phone to make a call, without ringing the operator. You could input the number then and call someone long distance without having to pay the outrageous prices. He was the precedent for a group of youths that helped people make long distance calls for free. This group was called Youth International Party Line/Technical Assistance Program (YIPL/TAP).

Phone hacking became so popular that the creators of Apple, Steve Jobs and Steve Wozniak, started out as phone hackers. They created the "Blue Boxes". These devices helped everyday people hack into the phone system without having to rely on anyone else.

The Milwaukee group the 414s were the first Federal arrests for hacking. In 1980, they were accused of hacking into over sixty computer systems all around their area. They broke into hospital records, and into many other big business information centers to gather credit card info.

In the late 1980s more laws were enacted against hacking, and more people got arrested. The Fry Guy was one, and he was called such due to the fact that he mainly hacked McDonalds' computer systems. Along with The Fry Guy, a group of people hacked the First National Bank of Chicago, and got away with seventy million dollars. Kevin Mitnick was arrested for hacking computer security software, and was charged with stealing software and damaging computers.

By the 1990s hacking was becoming a widespread problem. A group of hackers spread out all over the US were responsible for AT&T's service crashes on Martin Luther King Jr. Day. This started a national crackdown on hacking laws. However, that doesn't stop people from breaking into computer systems and stealing military documents, as Kevin Lee Poulsen did. A hacker was responsible for the death threats received by a Texas A&M professor as well. The unknown hacker logged onto his professor's computer from a different location and sent upwards of ten thousand racist emails using the professor's email. Kevin Mitnick was also seized again for hacking various systems.

However one of the best hacks of the early nineties was done by a sixteen year old hacker. "Data Stream", as he was called, broke into an air force base, NASA, and a Korean Atomic Research Institute, all remotely. The British teen curled up into the fetal position when sized by the Scotland Yard.

In the later 1990s Federal websites were defaced by hackers. Among those hacked were the Air Force, CIA, and NASA. The Canadians got in on the hacking scheme, when a fifteen year old boy broke into the Canadian Broadcasting Corp. site and post that "The Media are Liars" all over it. Microsoft and Yahoo were targeted as well. Microsoft was targeted to illustrate its new software's weaknesses, and Yahoo was targeted in an attempt to get Mitnick released from prison.

Mitnick supporters again plagued the nation with through the United Nation's Children Fund site, and they threaten a virtual

Holocaust if Mitnick is not released from prison. Of course, their bluff again did not work.

There are many other cases of hacking that made national news, but those are the most interesting of cases. As you can see, hacking has been around for a long time, and though it can be useful at times, it can also be very dangerous. It is a great power, and with great power comes great responsibility.

Difference Between Good and Bad Hacking

Ethical Hacking

Ethical hacking, or white hat hacking, is when a company hires a person to hack into their systems to find flaws. These hackers act with full rights and permissions to use their skills. They are often employed by an actual company that hires people to check out the security on their clients' sites. One of these companies is the CSC, or Computer Sciences Corporation)

There are several famous white hat hackers that made the changes in the internet you are still experiencing today. We wouldn't have half the technology we do today without these hackers, and though they are not spoke about as much as the famous black hat hackers, they are still very important.

Take Tim Berners-Lee for example. He was a hacker, and he used those skills to create the World Wide Web (WWW). He also created the HTML and URL systems. We still use these today, and I imagine, with how internet crazed everyone is, we use them quite frequently. Even though they have been updated since then the basic process is still the same one created by Berners-Lee.

Vinton Cerf, the father of the internet as we know it today, was a hacker, and he used his skills to give us all the wonderful internet options we have today. He took the basics of what Berners-Lee did and expanded on it, and made it better and faster.

There are many other white hat hackers that have created systems and computer languages that we find crucial today. PERL would not have existed without the hacker Larry Wall. PERL is a programming language that is used for many different computer tasks.

Unethical hacking

Unethical hacking, or black hat hacking, is what you mainly hear about in the news. A criminal hacks into a computer system and steals money. Some teenager hacks his schools firewall and places pictures of various exploitative material all over the home page. It seems for every one white hat hacker, there are two black hat hackers. This can cause all of hacking to be painted in a bad light, when that's not the case. A few bad apples, however, do tend to give an entire group a bad name.

Black hat hacking consists of mainly breaking into computer systems because someone wants to break the rules. It gives them a rush to know they have the power to control one of the most expansive databases of information. Scratch that, THE most expansive database for information. There are some black hats though that actually hack to steal people's information, and to steal money.

Kevin Mitnick is one of these people. He has hacked many databases to steal money, and corrupt files. He has been caught several times in his life, and once was caught by a group of white hat hackers. Major plot twist there. After he went to prison, his legacy lived on with hacker groups threatening virtual holocausts if he wasn't released from prison. None of their attempts worked.

Most of you reading this may have heard about the group Anonymous. They have been around for a while, but are slowly gaining more power in the hacking world. While none of their hacking is malicious, they often encourage civil unrest, and disobedience in the hopes of starting riots and overthrowing the government. As of late, they have been known for releasing sealed documents to the public concerning government officials and their illegal and illicit activities.

Black hat hackers are everywhere. They often attack through spam emails, and virus infected downloads. These allow them into your computer, and into your personal information. They can use this to create identity fraud.

Identity fraud is one of the biggest things that hackers do. As of late it seems like the main purpose of black hat hackers. They take a person's identity, and open new credit card accounts, and bank accounts. They can drive a person thousands of dollars into debt in just a year. This hacking is severely unethical, and should not be done for any reason. It is one of the most punishable hacking crimes there is and gets the second longest amount of jail time underneath hacking federal systems. However, people still do it, knowing the risks.

My dear readers, please do not fall into this tempting trap. I know the purpose of this book is to teach you all about hacking, and the steps to begin, but the purpose is for the intention of white hat hacking. Please do not become a black hat hacker. It isn't worth the jail time. A lot of black hat hackers started out with the intention of becoming a white hat hacker, very few make it that far. They get a dose of power, and it corrupts them. Hacking is a wonderful thing, do not abuse it, for its true power only shows its head in the hands of a white hat hacker.

Chapter 2: Things to Learn Before You Begin

Hacking is not something you can just watch a YouTube video and become a master at. You have to do some research on things before you begin. The basics of these things will be covered in this chapter, but the more you research them, the better understanding you will have in the field of hacking.

As with any topic, there are some basic things you should know before you get started. In hacking you should know about common network protocols, network ports, firewalls, and computer networks. Knowing more about these things will make it easier for you to understand the basics of hacking, and give you a good foundation to start from.

Computer Networking

This is what allows computers to share data through a telecommunications network. They use a data link that can be transmitted through a cable or wirelessly. The best known one is the internet, which many of us use daily. The devices that originate these signals are called network nodes. They can have hosts such as phone networks or home computers. Computer networks host a number of different services, and is often considered electrical engineering since it uses practical and theoretical application of related disciplines.

There are many different sub categories of networking, but to list them would draw away from the point of this book, and distract you from the processes you need to know. However, a quick internet search will give you more information on these sub categories should you be interested in learning more.

Firewalls

Firewalls are a basic protection from viruses and other malware that most software programs use nowadays. A firewall monitors information coming and leaving the host internal network. Firewalls have many layers that you would have to break through to hack, and in these layers are sub layers that are even trickier to hack into.

Network Ports

These are the endpoints of data communication. This is where you want to get to when hacking. They are what identify a specific process or service. They are connected to a sixteen bit code known as a port number. Each port number is unique to the specific process, not a specific device. This makes it easier to identify a service by using one of the one thousand and twenty four port numbers out there for major products. From there, there are specific sub-ports to choose from to identify a specific branch of a service. These are called transmission controlled protocols. TCP for short.

IP Addresses

IP addresses (Internet Protocol Addresses) are numerical labels assigned to each specific device that is part of a computer network that uses internet protocols. When it was first designed, it was a 32-bit label known as IPV4 but as the network has grown over the years, it has changed and become a 128-bit label known as IPV6. The IP address is assigned by the IANA (Internet Assigned Numbers Authority), and re-allocated to different internet providers. They are assigned based on the type of network and size of the processor.

Hypertext Transfer Protocol

Hypertext transfer protocol, or HTTP, is the data communication foundation for the world wide web. HTTP uses logical links, otherwise known as hyperlinks, to exchange hypertext between network nodes. The first version, created by Tim Berners-Lee, was dubbed HTTP/1.1. It became obsolete in 1999 but wasn't upgraded fully until 2015 when HTTP/2 came out.

HTTP functions in the client-server computing model as a request-response protocol. The client requests information (a web page generally) and the server provides the data requested. HTTP allows intermediate networks to communicate better with the internet world.

HTTP serves many different purposes, and it would take forever to list them all, and would distract from the purpose of this book. A quick search will give you more in depth info on the subject.

Another good idea is to find a few good sources of learning material before you start hacking. Along with this book it is best to have one or two more pieces of learning material to read to grasp a better understanding of things that are only skimmed over on here. More materials will be added towards the end of this book to give you a good idea of what would be good to read for a beginner.

Chapter 3: Programming

Programming is not necessary to hack, but if you know programming, it will make you a better hacker. This chapter will go over, in depth, the basics of programming. If you know about programming, and can do it well, you can write your own programs for hacking, rather than rely on hacking packets that can be a little buggy. Some people go with those packets, but they never move past the beginner level of hacking. Programmers can become expert hackers, and often get the hang of hacking a lot faster than someone who has had minimal knowledge of the world of computer language.

What is Programming?

Programming is the act of instructing a computer to do your bidding by inputting a code in the computer's language so that it can understand the task at hand. You formulate a plan to a computing problem, and turn it into an executable program. It involves generating algorithms, developing analysis understanding and verification of algorithms. You have to make sure they are correct, because just one simple mistake could cause your program not to run.

In programming, you need to find a secret of commands that will get the computer to do what you want, and instruct it to do a specific task, or fix a problem. You can use programming for a variety of things, such as source code, testing, debugging, computer programs, software and much, much more.

Programming is an instrumental phase of software engineering. It is also considered an art, an engineering discipline, and a craft. Many people say it can only be one of those things, but in reality, it is all of those things. Programming is a beautiful, technical art that requires great patience, but if you have that patience, it is easy to learn.

In programming your code has to be pretty easy to read, if you want to reach the average person. However, your code can be more complex if it a program for advanced computer aficionados. However, since you are learning the basics of hacking in this book, we will stick to the basics of programming.

Programming readability is not only important because people heave to read it, but the longer the code, the more vulnerable it becomes to bugs, and mistakes in the code when writing it out. It also makes it harder for other programmers to find out where the problem is originating from. The simpler the code, the easier it is to understand it.

However, programming is not just about understanding and reading the code. There are many other parts of programming you should know. These parts are the less talked about, but crucially essential part of programming that make it tick.

Programming Language

Before you learn how to program, you must first learn about programming languages. These are how you communicate with the program, and the foundation on which you build your program.

Programming languages are formal languages or constructed languages that computers use to instruct a machine to do its bidding.

It is specifically used to create computer programs, however the first programmable item preceded the computer by over a hundred years. It was a programmable flute from Islam's Golden age.

A program language must follow some key elements. These elements allow the computer to understand the program. If a computer can't understand what it needs to do it won't do it. These elements are as follows:

Function and Target

A computer has to perform some kind of computation for any task involving the computer itself, or an algorithm for an external device. These devices can be something such as a phone, a printer, or a fax machine. There are programs that are used to control a display on a TV or projector as well. You can write a computer program to control almost any electronic device.

The language in these programs have to be functional, and efficient. They have to get the message across quickly, and the longer your program is language-wise, the longer it takes for the computer or device to read it and communicate properly. If there is a mistake it may not reach its target, and would not work properly. Your program has to be functional and precise, therefore simplicity is always the best option.

Abstractions and Excessive Power

A program often includes abstractions to instruct the computer to do all it is capable of doing rather than just the bare minimum. These customized abstractions allow the program to manipulate data structures or control the flow of information. This is called the abstraction principle.

Another part of abstractions is the computing power the fullest extent it can express. To do this you often use all Turing complete languages, or ones that are not fully complete but still considered Turing programming languages. An example of complete verses incomplete would be complete:XSLT and LaTex or incomplete:XML or HTML.

Programming language and computer language are terms that are often interchangeable, however they are slightly different, and that difference changes amongst users. One generally refers to just programming, the other refers to the whole system. And it generally is different among people which is which.

Program Language Names

Just like we as humans have different languages, computers have different languages as well, though unlike us, these languages are not region-specific, rather, they are intention-specific. While I am going to name all the languages, this section will focus on the most versatile and popular language, C++.

The languages are as follows:

A-L

ActionScript

ALGOL

ADA

AIML

Assembly

AutoHotKey

Babel

BASIC

BatchFile

BCPL

Brooks

C

C#

C++

Clojure

COBOL

CoffeeScript

CPL

Curl

Curry

D

DarkBASIC

dBASE

Dylan

F

F#

FORTRAN

FoxPro

GO

GW Basic

Haskell

HDML

HTML

Java

JavaScript

JCL

Julia

LISP

LiveScript

LOGO

Lua

M-Z

MatLab

MUMPS

Nim

Objective-C

Pascal

PERL

PHP

Pick

Pure Basic

Python

Prolog

QBasic

R

Racket

Reia

Ruby

Rust

Scala

Scheme

SGML

Simula

SmallTalk

SQL

TCL

TurboPascal

True Basic

VHDL

Visual Basic

Visual FoxPro

WML

WHTML

XML

There are many things you can use these languages for, but not all of them work for everything. I will list a few of the most popular ones so you can get an idea of which language you would need to run for the type of hacking you would be doing. The most popular, C++ will be covered later on in this chapter. Some of the things you can use program languages and what languages work for what is as follows:

Application and Program Development

Internet browsers and other things you often use on a daily basis are considered programs. Here are some languages that will help you write your own program.

C

C++

Java

Visual Basic

Artificial Intelligence Development-

This is what makes robots interact without human instruction. It is also the computer playing you in a game. It is a decision making development. To write AI here are some languages that would help.

C++

Prolog

AIML

There are many other things you can use languages for, such as gaming and database development, internet and script development, and computer drivers. When you decide on a type of programming you would like to get into, you can decide the language that is right for you. For now we are going to work on program development with C++.

Creating a Program with C++

This seven step tutorial is not all-inclusive but will give you the beginning knowledge you need to traverse out on your own into the wonderful world of programming. Of course you will need a little background information with every step, so along with each step there will be a little information on what the step entails and a basic way to go about the step. Some steps may be longer than others, but every step is important. I will also include a link at the bottom to direct you to a website that will teach you more about C++ for free. It is a course on C++ that will guide you through from the basics to the advanced levels. Feel free to take a look at that if C++ interests you. But anyways, let's get down to business.

The best way to learn something is to first learn how it came to be, and its roots. This will help you understand some of the finer points, such as object-oriented programming. Well, I doubt you want to search all over the web for the history of C++, I mean after all this is supposed to be a ultimate guide to hacking, so I will include the important parts of C++'s history.

History of C++

In 1979, Bjarne Strousup was doing some research for his Doctorate thesis, and he began to work with a Simula variant, called The Simula 67 Language. This was regarded as the first object-oriented supporting language. Strousup was intrigued by this useful programing language, and wanted to develop from it, and make it better, as it was far too slow for practical use.

From there he began to work on C with Classes. This was meant to be a superset of object-oriented language, that didn't sacrifice speed for functionality. His program included all classes, inlining, basic inheritance, and default function arguments along with all the other functions of the C languages.

Derived from a C compiler called Cpre, Strousup was able to create the first C compiler with classes known as Cfront. This self-hosting compiler was supposed to translate all the C with classes language to just the C language. However, by 1993 this was abandoned as it was too difficult to add new features onto, making it obsolete. However, despite being obsolete, it made a big impact and was a major breakthrough for the programming languages.

In 1983 a new incrementing value was implemented into C with Classes, making it C++. During this time, many new features were added, and it was re-vamped for better use.

In 1985, C++ was released as a commercial product, and sold to the public for use, though the language was not yet standardized. This made the book on C++ a very important reference. This book was written by Stroussup, and was the first reference he made to C++ being an actual programming language.

In 1990, an annotated C++ reference manual was released to the public, and in that same year a turbo C++ compiler was released to the public for sale. This compiler added a plethora of additional libraries to the regular C++ compiler, all while running nearly ten times faster. This compiler is still used in many places today.

In 1998, C++ finally got its first international standards. This standard is formally known as C++98. The full length title is C++ ISO/IEC 14882:1998. (click the link to learn more). The annotated reference manual for C++ was said to be the biggest influence towards the standard. They also included the Standard Template Library, which was instrumental in its success. However, it was revised in 2003 to fix some problems the outdated 98 version had. They dubbed this revision C++03

In 2005 a major revision began on the C++ standards. While it was expected to be released before the end of the first decade in the new millennium, it wasn't released till 2011. They released updates until then.

In 2011, the new standard of C++ was finally released. It was titled, you guessed it, C++11. The driving impact on the release was the Boos Library Project. This new C++ was faster, and more reliable than the others, with more features and library modules.

So there you have it. A brief history on C++. Hopefully you will understand more about the language, and be able to continue on in these steps with ease.

Step Two

Install a C++ compiler

A compiler is necessary as it puts all of the language into a folder that your computer can run. Visual C++ is a good one as it already has an independent development environment (IDE for short) built in. An IDE makes writing source code easier.

Visual C++

This is a compiler issued by Visual Studios Express, a Microsoft tool that creates many compilers for different computer languages. You can download a free compressed version from http://www.microsoft.com/express/. The one you would need to download would be Express for Windows Desktop.

You can run the application after installing it by following the instructions on the installer. Once installed, it will have a range of support for many languages including C++11 both the full and free version are designed to build a variety of applications.

To compile and run Visual Express

- Open Visual Express
- Click file
- Select run
- On the left hand side, select templates
- Chose Visual C++
- In the central area choose Win32 Console Application
- On the bottom partition, name the file and select file location
- wait for the Win32 Application Wizard to pop up
- Click next
- Leave Console Application Marked
- Mark Empty Project
- Click finish
- Find Solution Explorer on the right
- Chose File Solution
- Right click
- Chose add

- Select New Item

- Add a new C++ file

- Name it with a .cpp extension (Example.cpp)

- Click ok

- When the editor pops up add this to it line by line

```
1. #include <iostream>
2. int main()
3. {
4.    auto x = R"(Hello world!)";
5.    std::cout << x;
6. }
```

- Compile and run by pressing Ctr+F5

Step Three

Chose a Tutorial

This is a very important step, as you need to know how to run C++ properly. As this guide is just an overview, it does not contain everything you need to know, merely the basics. A tutorial can help you further your knowledge of the subject, and make you a better programmer, and when you become a better programmer, you can become a better hacker. There are many different tutorials out there, but most cost money, and you have to pay for individual lessons. My favorite all inclusive tutorial is more like a course on C++ and it is free. http://www.learncpp.com/ Follow the link and begin to learn more about C++ and become a master.

Step Four

Try Out Each Concept

There are many different concepts that you can try. You can even try to create your own. You can go the copy-and-paste route, but it will only get you so far. To maximize what you learned, try creating your own programs using what you have learned.

Step Five

Learn From Others

There is always going to be someone better than you at different parts of programming. That is the great thing. You can always find someone you can learn from to better yourself. Look for weak areas in your programming skills and find someone who excels in those areas. Learn from them, and adapt their knowledge to your advantage.

Step Six

Work through Problems

Using the skills you have learned, find some demo problems online. These will help you sharpen your skills and apply them to real situations. It is always best to find a wide variety of problems to practice on, because the wider the range your skills are, the better you will be.

Step Seven

Help Others

The best way to ensure that you retain all the information you have learned, is to help someone else learn the program. This walks you back through everything, and the more you do it, the more comfortable you will get with your abilities as a programmer.

These are the steps to becoming a programmer so that you can better learn hacking skills, and step outside the already existing hacking source packets.

Chapter 4: More Knowledge on Hacking

I can imagine you thought that now that you know how to program, we would move onto how to hack. However we are not ready to get to that yet. Programming was just one of the things you needed to know to become a successful hacker. The more you know about the subject, the better you will become at it, and there is still a lot of information to learn about before we get to hacking itself. Be patient, as we will get to it all in due time.

Classifications of Hacking

You already heard about white and black hat hackers, however there are many different classifications of hackers, and they all do different things. Just like many things hacking is not only black and white.

White Hats-

These people are the ones who graduated Yale with a masters degree in IT training, and use their powers only for good. They hack a business website and find all the flaws that need fixed so that the website will be the best it can be. Think all the stereotypical nerds you see engrossed in their computers on TV and in movies. Those are the white hat hackers. The ones that are always swept up in a scheme and are trying to be the moral compass. "Guys this isn't what I use my abilities for. Its… illegal. I am a legal hacker, nothing more." Yet he gets persuaded by the pretty girl to do what he really doesn't want to. Those are generally the white hats. Sometimes though, once they get that taste of illegal power, they turn into the next classification of hackers.

Black Hats-

These bad guys are out for power, and want to help no one but themselves. These are the villains that steal your identity, and run you up thousands of dollars in credit card debt. These guys are the ones you see involved in twenty first century bank robberies on the news. These evil people are the reason that hackers have a bad name. All it takes is a few bad apples to soil an entire batch, and these people are definitely bad apples. Often times they started out as white hat hackers who got a taste of power, and fell into the darkness of black hat hacking. These people go after databases of information, and crack into thousands of accounts at one time. They often bounce their signals off of multiple towers to make it hard to find them, so they are also hard to catch.

Grey Hats-

These guys fall in the middle of the Black and White hat hackers. They are not doing their hacking for personal gains, but their hacking could still be considered illegal and unethical. If you have ever seen the hit TV show NCIS on CBS then you are probably familiar with their character, Timothy McGee. He is considered a grey hat hacker, because he uses his hacking skills in illegal ways to obtain information to help them stop a criminal. He often hacks into sealed FBI records, or other federal government sealed databases and acquires the information needed. If caught he could be in a lot of trouble, but he is doing it for the greater good, and that is what grey hat hacking is. Surprisingly grey hats are the largest group of hackers there is. Most hackers do illegal things for the greater good.

Red Hats-

These guys are like the bounty hunters of the hacking world. They hunt down the black hat hackers and bring them to justice. They follow the bad hacker's trails and bring them down. They have no tolerance for black hat hackers and unlike white hats, they act of their own accord and are not hired to find these criminals.

Blue Hats-

Think blue collar workers. That is basically what these guys are in the hacking industry. They are generally hired by Microsoft to find bugs in a program that Microsoft doesn't own and report to Microsoft. These guys generally create anti-malware programs.

Elite Hackers-

These guys are the hacking gods and goddesses of the hacking world. They generally don't hack for a specific purpose other than to raise their skill level in the playing field. These hackers are some of the most talented hackers there are and very few make it to the Elite level.

Hacktivists-

These guys are the ones who expose things, or hack for a moral reason. They are trying to promote a cause or a religion, or whatever campaign they have in mind. There are two types of hacktivists. There are the cyber-terrorists, and the freedom hacktivists.

Cyber-Terrorists

These guys use their abilities to deface and destroy databases as leverage to get what they want. They are like the Al-Qaeda of the internet world. While they are not able to physically harm people, they can take down power grids, or launch a virus to take down the entire internet. However, they are generally bluffing, and not many people fall for their ruse.

Freedom Hacktivists

These people expose information that governments have been hiding from their people. The famous hacking group, Anonymous, is one of these freedom groups. They expose things about politicians to try to get the world to see the truth and stand up for their freedom. Often, if caught, they are convicted of treason, and thrown in jail for life. They risk their lives to bring information that the world needs to know to light.

Nation State Hackers

Government sanctioned hackers that use their abilities to start cyber-warfare. They are often from other countries trying to spy on their enemies government. This type of espionage is highly frowned upon by the UN but is not illegal, and it pays pretty well, considering the only thing being risked is your reputation.

Neophytes

Also called green hats. They are people who have just got into learning about hacking. They do not have many skills but are steadily learning more, to become full-fledged hackers.

Script Kiddies

These people just do it for the thrill. They are not hacking for any reason other than to say they can. They often do not have many skills and use hack packages rather than writing their own code.

Those are the classifications of hackers that are out there. Once you decide what classification you want to be, you can adapt your hacking skills accordingly. But stay away from black hat hacking. That is some dangerous, and very bad stuff.

Types of Hacking

Hacking is an all-inclusive term for many different activities done by hackers. The type of activities depends on what type of hacker is doing the hacking. For this section we will focus on the two main groups. Black and white hacking.

White Hat Hacking-

There are several activities that a white hat hacker does to test the security of a program. Such as:

Penetration Tests:

Ethical hackers are hired to run what is often called a PenTest on a system to check for bugs and loopholes. There are many different sources they use to do this.

Software Framework:

A customizable software that provides generic functions for a hacker to use. There are a few favorites among hackers and they are as follows:

- Metasploit Project
- w3af

- NMAP

- Burp Project

- OWASP Zap

Specialized Operating System Distributions

Pre-packaged tools to operate a PenTest. There are several available, such as:

- Kali Linux

- Pentoo

- WHAX

A PenTest verifies points of entry, and the hackers try to use these to enter the system. Then they report their findings to the company.

Along with PenTests, white hat hackers also use all the means that black hat hackers do to find loopholes and close them.

Black Hat Hacking-

These guys do a lot of different types of hacking, just like white hats, only difference is one is for good one is for evil. White hats do everything a black hat does, but a black hat does not do everything a white hat does. They only do the illegal stuff, such as:

Phishing-

This is a type of hacking that uses a legitimate company's name to gain information. They usually try to gain personal information like credit card information, social security number, and personal stats (age birth date, etc).

There are many ways that a phisher will use to try to gain information.

- Malware is one of the biggest problems when it comes to compromising your personal information. It sneaks into your computer through a seemingly harmless download. This download is fraught with viruses that steal your information and send it back to the hacker.

- Search Engines are another way that phishers steal information. You get on a search engine that looks real, but it has spyware on it. Whenever you go to input a password on a site or buy something with your card, the spyware send that information back to the phisher, and they can chose to use it as they see fit.

- Instant Messages are sent between the phisher and the user. The phisher sends the user a fake link that looks real and when you click on the link you are asked to input sensitive information. This information is then stolen by the phisher for their personal use.

- Web based phishing is where a phisher uses a midway point to steal your information from a legitimate site. This sophisticated type of phishing is so discreet, you won't even know what's going on.

- Spam emails are also a way to steal information. You open the email and it asks you to urgently verify your account to make some money or some other detail like that. To verify your account you have to input your SSN and generally you have to buy something as well.

Imitation Wireless Access Points-

These access points are created by the phisher to gain any information transmitted across the wireless connection. This WAP often asks you to create a log-in profile to use it as well to gain access to more sensitive information. These access points often gather Intel on your social media accounts and credit card information.

UI Redress Attacks, or Clickjacking is where the user thinks he or she is clinking on a real link, but is instead clicking on an layer that sends the info to the hacker instead. So while they think they could be inputting their info onto their bank's website, really they just got their information stolen.

Cookie theft has been around as long as there has been internet. The internet stores your information in the form of cookies, this information includes passwords, the websites you visit, and all the information you put into those websites. This is an ongoing war between white and black hat hackers, as every time a white hat creates more security, a black hat finds a way around it.

DoS attacks, or Denial of Service attacks, are not phishing schemes. Rather they are attacks that distract the websites owners while doing even more damage than just stealing one person's information. These attacks can last for weeks, and leave a website inoperable for legitimate users, while the hackers do their nefarious deeds. These can damage the company's reputations as well as cost them a loss in revenue, and damage the company's website as well. These highly public attacks are common amongst hacktivists.

DDos attacks are called Distributed Denial of service attacks in which the denial of service attack comes from many computers rather than just one. They are otherwise just like a DoS attack.

Those are the most popular types of hacking that black hat hackers use. A couple more you could look up if you want to do more research would be pharming, keystroke logging, SQL injecting and packet sniffing. These ones are less popular but still highly effective in the world of black hat hacking.

Computer Viruses

These are a computer user's worst nightmare. The most dreaded term you could ever hear is "your computer has a virus". Viruses can be costly to fix, and the spread so rapidly that generally there is quite a few before you even know they are there. By the time you get your computer looked at, all your important information has been compromised, and your console is so virus ridden that it would be cheaper to buy a new one than to clear the viruses off your old one. Never leave a virus on your computer thinking it is harmless. This is one of the biggest mistakes you can make and it can be very costly. Over sixty eight percent of money lost to viruses is unrecoverable.

There are many types of viruses that a hacker uses, knowing them will allow you to protect yourself from them as you engage on your hacking adventures. (Yes hackers get viruses too)

- Memory Resident Virus- These viruses are evil nasty ones that sit in your computer's memory, and wake up and run when the system is turned on. They send all the information that is tagged back to the hacker.

- Polymorphic viruses- This virus changes every time it infects a system so no two viruses are the same. This makes it harder to be discovered by anti-virus software as it doesn't have the same code strings as other viruses do.

- Direct Action Viruses- These are weak little viruses that are easy for an anti-virus scanner to detect and delete. They hide in a hard drive root file and replicate themselves every time certain criteria is met and activates it.

- Macro viruses- They infect the macros on your computer, and are generally transmitted through emails. They affect things like word documents and the templates surrounding them. The easiest way to avoid these is to not open emails from unknown senders, even if they are in your primary folder and not in your spam folder.

- Fat Viruses- These can be some of the most destructive viruses to your computer. They hide in file space and corrupt important files that affect the consoles interoperability. Run advanced security scans often to protect against these viruses, also scan anything you plug into your computer, such as a flash drive.

- Overwrite virus- These files do exactly what the name states. It infects files and overwrites the data in them without changing the file size. You have no idea the virus is there unless you go to use the file.

- MultiPartite virus- These viruses are tricky as they operate multiple ways, and there is no single way to activate them. To get rid of them, you have to wipe the entire hard drive, and reload the information. Be sure to scan everything you reload.

Computer viruses are nasty things and they can cause a lot of damage to a computer, however, you can avoid getting a lot of them by using common sense, and never operating a computer without an anti-virus protection on the console.

How to Protect Yourself

1. Secure your home network. This is where you will do most of your most sensitive searching, and input the most personal information. It only makes sense that you would lock down your home network so that people can't access the information you send across it.

2. Avoid sketchy sites, as these are a harbor for all sorts of nasty viruses and malware. You can download Norton to check if a website is secure or not.

3. Do not fall for pop-up scams. If your browser pops up saying that you are infected, ignore it. This is a scam. Your anti-virus will alert you if you are at risk. These pop ups are meant to scare users into downloading virus ridden software claiming it is a security feature for your computer.

4. Be careful opening email attachments, as these are a common vessel for viruses. Only open attachments from a person you trust, otherwise you could put your computer at a high risk.

5. Stay away from ads. These can land you in a heap of virus and malware trouble. If you see something truly intriguing, find a legitimate website instead of clicking the ad. This can protect you from hackers stealing your information.

6. Stay away from free wifi and the cloud. These two things are like shining beacons for hackers, and they love to attack these two things, as so many people are inputting information at one time. If you must use these two things, do not add any information that could aid a hacker in stealing your identity.

7. Protect your passwords. Never let anyone know your password to anything. They can use this information to learn your passwords to everything else, especially if you are a predictable person. Also make sure you use a different password for every site, and that your password is strong, and hard to crack. These precautions will protect you in a lot of areas.

8. Password protect everything, and remove all personal info when selling an item. You should even have a pass code on your phone and tablet. This will keep people from opening up your personal info. Also, wipe the device completely when selling something. This removes all traces of personal info, and protects you from people stealing your identity.

9. When in doubt change everything. Change your password to any site you think might be compromised, and if you think it is your computer, wipe it, and start again. This prevents you from having too much damage from viruses.

Follow these tips to prevent yourself from becoming victim to hackers and viruses. If you keep your computer clean, you will be able to focus more time on hacking and less time on cleaning up another hacker's mess.

Terms You Should Know

There are many terms you should know in your hacking journey. These terms will help you along your way, and aid you in further understanding of the hacking profession.

- Back Door- A trap door of sorts that allows a hacker in without a password

- Bot- A program that runs automatically. Commonly used as a tool in DoS hacking. Also can refer to a hijacked computer used on BotNet

- BotNet- a group of computers being hijacked. The owners of these computers do not know what is going on. Common tactic in DoS attacks, and was a popular tactic of the Soviet Union in the war.

- Brute Force Attack- an inefficient way of hacking that uses a tool to find every possible password for a specific system.

- C Programming Language- Extremely popular programming language amongst hackers. Used primarily for applications and programming.

- Code- Generally a text based language for machines used to instruct the computer to do a task.

- Cookie- An information storing byte on the internet to make the web more user friendly. Also a common target for hacker attacks.

- Doxing- a technique that uses both the use of public social media information and hacking and stalking to find anonymous information and publish it in your own name.

- Encryption- Requires a key to access sensitive information. This is an effective security measure on sensitive files.

- Glitch- A disruption of a program or equipment.

- IP- The specific fingerprint that identifies your device on the internet. Stands for Internet Protocol Address

- Kernel- also known as the nucleus. It controls everything that goes on in a computer.

- Linux- an open-source operating system based on UNIX.

- Malware- An information hijacking program that enters your computer through a variety of ways, and leaves destruction in its wake.

- Proxy- the middle man on a server. Can be used for anonymity as well as bypassing controls.

- Root Kit- a hacker's tool to getting in to control a system whilst remaining undetected.

- Spyware- piggybacks onto malware to send information it finds back to the hacker.

- SQL- The major programming language to send information back to data bases.

- TCP- a protection safeguard that scans information and does safety checks on the internet. The web relies highly on this safeguard.

- Trojan Horse- A gift with a nasty surprise. It delivers a download but also installs viruses and spyware on your computer.

- UDP- one of the core members of the IPC, and it uses simple transmissions models.

- UNIX- one of the oldest programming models there is. It is very popular and can reach multiple systems.

- Zombie- A hijacked computer on BotNet

There are some terms as well that you will need to fit in to the hacker scene. These terms are not actual definitions, but rather, a slang that hackers across the world use.

- Bit Rot- The term for files that erode over time due to continuous use. Even unused files degrade over time.

- CopyBroke- A corrupted copyright program that has been damaged due to a bug or bit rot.

- Crayola. A mini computer that rivals a super computer but is a lot less expensive.

- Cruft- one of the oldest terms in hacker slang, referring to a garbage code that is long and redundant.

- Dinosaur- very old hardware or conservative computer user.

- Easter Egg- a pleasant surprise hidden in the code, such as a joke, snatch of music, or famous person's name. These make code writing, and reading, a little more pleasant.

- Finger- an indicator of who has visited a program. Usually contains terminal used, username, and time visited.

- Hacked off- a term that means irritated or angry. Can also refer to someone who thinks their code will be used for criminal activity.

- Sandbox- This is a term for the research and development phase of a program. The term "go play in the sandbox" means "go work on this some more" in hacking terms.

- Spaghetti code- a long twisted and tangled code that is severely unstructured.

Hacker Culture

This is a small group of hackers that enjoy creatively and persistently overcoming obstacles in the hacker world. These are the hackers that often make it into the class of elite hackers. They often do what they do for the challenge and the respect. They do what has never been done before, and move on to the next thing as if it is no big deal.

Hackers often seem antisocial, but writing code is lonely work. You have to spend hours in front of a computer and continuously look for breaks in your program to make it better. This is not a conducive lifestyle for attending lavish parties, and being super social. Most hackers don't really make friends in the outside world, because they constantly have to turn down invitations to hang out. However, they do make friends online. These friends don't pressure them to go out, and they can swap secrets to hacking, and share information they find.

Despite the media portraying all hackers as black hat hackers, most are not. Most hackers only do so to say they could. They view as an athlete views the world record. Something to beat to earn major bragging rights. Ninety percent of hackers have no intent of doing anything malicious with their abilities, rather, they just want to break into secure systems to say they can.

Hackers love to learn new things, so they are all for open-source programs. These programs allow anyone access to alter or change something in a program to make it better. Doing so helps other hackers learn new things they may not have already known. They learn from experience and adapt on their findings. Hackers are very knowledgeable people, and they love to share their information.

Hacker is a loose term that also covers crackers. Crackers are people who hack with malicious intent. This allows the media to portray all hackers as no good evildoers, and label them as untrustworthy. This is hardly the case. Most hackers hate that they are associated with black hats just because they consider themselves hackers.

Hackers stay in touch in a variety of ways, such as camps and events that are held yearly. There is also a journal regularly published called *The Hacker's Quarterly*. This journal provides information on findings in the hacking community, and recommendations for newer software. There are also online sites that hackers post their info on, and they have games and puzzles to help strengthen your hacking skills.

There are a few things to remember if you want to join the hacking community. All information should be exchanged freely, always have a good attitude about the task you are planning on taking on, always believe that computers make your life easier, and believe in yourself. Follow these principles, and you will fit right in to the hacking community.

Chapter 5: Hacking and the Law

It is pertinent to remember that all hacking is illegal, unless you are sanctioned to do so by a company or the government. Most law enforcement do not care for hackers due to the fact that they can break into classified information should the mood ever strike them. They consider hackers a thorn in their side, a nuisance that will not be tolerated unless given their sanction. So at all costs avoid getting caught when dabbling in hacking. They don't care if your intentions were not malicious, they will treat you as a criminal anyway.

There are many laws that are put in place to attempt to keep people away from hacking, and depending on the sensitivity of the information you are obtaining, the repercussions are not favorable. You could be slapped with hefty fines, probation, or even jail. The crimes range from a class b misdemeanor to a class b felony. If you are caught hacking into a government database, then you might as well kiss your life goodbye. They will pin you with as many charges as they possibly can, and the lowest sentence there is twenty years in prison. Every other charge after that can add ten to twenty years on your sentence, and they generally make you serve them consecutively, so you could be looking at life in prison.

Most hacking crimes are prosecuted under the CFAA act or the Wire Tap Act. These are two very serious crimes. Along with these, there is the Unlawful Access to Stored Communications Act, Identity Theft and Aggravated Identity theft, Access Device Fraud, Can-Spam Act, Wire Fraud and Communications interference.

Also, each state has its own parameters for charging hackers with crimes. Some states are stricter than even the federal level, so it is best to check the laws in your state as well to be prepared. Charges add up fast. It is best to stay one step ahead of the game.

Hacking a computer in another country is a process you definitely do not want to get caught doing. Some countries will not hesitate to execute you, and many won't allow extradition of the case to your home country, as even though you committed the crime in your own living room, the crime physically happened on their soil.

Keep all this information in mind as you dabble in hacking. There are ways to help avoid getting caught and it is best to employ them. That will be talked about in a later chapter.

Basic skills to become a hacker

- Basic Computer skills- This is a no-brainer, but it should still be said that you need basic computer skills. This expands more past being able to surf the web and use Microsoft office proficiently, you must also be able to run command prompts and set up networking systems. You do not have to be a genius, but you need to have some skill in how to work a computer beyond its basic functions.

- Networking Skills- You have to be able to understand networking as well. This includes understanding:

--DHCP- Dynamic Host Configuration Protocol. This is a networking protocol used for IP networks. It is controlled by servers that distribute services, interfaces, and IP addresses. Routers can be used as DHCP servers. Without DHCP services, every device has to be assigned an IP address manually.

A DHCP server can manipulate and instruct information coming from TCP/IP settings. It automatically generates and assigns IP addresses to devices on its network. Routers receive a globally unique address and sub divide it amongst the devices on its network to make locally unique IP addresses.

When a device connects to a DHCP network, the router sends a query and requests necessary information from said device, and any server on the network can answer that request. DHCP servers not only manage multiple IP addresses, but also multiple domains and server types.

A single DHCP server can only service a large network when aided by relays. These relays have agents that send messages amongst the relays and back to the DHCP server mainframe.

There are three types of ways a DHCP can allocate an IP address

- Automatic Allocation- This is a permanent IP address assignment from the server. The DHCP keeps a table of IP addresses and notes the one the device had so every time it is rebooted on the server it maintains the same address that it had before.

☐ Dynamic Allocation- Each device has a range of IP addresses that are assigned to it. These addresses are reassigned when the device reboots on the network and requests an IP address from the server.

☐ Manual Allocation- This requires the administrator to map MAC addresses, and assign their own IP address on a private network, as the DHCP server is disabled. This feature has various names depending on what the router's name is.

DHCP's service model is a user datagram protocol, UDP for short. It uses two port numbers, port 67 and port 68. 67 is assigned to the server, and 68 is assigned to the client. It operates in a set of four stages known as DORA, or Server Discovery, IP Lease Offer, IP Lease Request, and IP Lease Acknowledgment.

☐ DHCP Discovery- The client broadcasts onto the server using destination address. The client may request the last IP address allocated to the device, but to be granted a request, the client must stay on the server. Otherwise, it will be allocated an IP address readily available, and the history of its former address will not be verified.

☐ DHCP offer- When the server receives the request it makes an offer on an IP address, Mac address, and every other bit of information the computer needs to get connected to the server. The address offer is based on the clients hardware address.

- DHCP request- Once the client receives the offer, it will request to lease the offered address. A client may choose from many offers but can only pick one. Once the client chooses an offer, the other servers withdraw theirs, and place them back in the list of available addresses.

- DHCP acknowledgment- Once the request is reviewed by the server, it then assigns the address to the client, and all the information needed. Once this is done, the client is set up and ready to go.

All of this is done in a few minutes of your first entering the server's network. Sometimes it takes even less time than that. It is amazing how fast information travels over a wireless connection. It travels across molecules you can't even see, sending more information than our brains can comprehend in a matter of seconds. It is inconceivable how much information is sent back and forth in the time it takes for you to connect to the Wi-Fi you are using. Truly magnificent.

There are many other factors that tie into the DHCP servers as well such as

- Vendor Identification- You can choose to identify the client or server by using a string of characters that would mean something to the client or server. One method to do this is to install a vendor class identifier. This allows the server to differentiate between two modems, and allow it to gain access to the functionality of a device.

- DHCP relaying- In small networks, a client can communicate directly with a server, but on a big network, a server needs relays to communicate between client and server. The broadcast is sent to a local link, where relays pick it up, and information is sent back the same way. The relay stores its own IP addresses and sends them to the servers using Unicast.

☐ Reliability- DHCP stays reliable by renewing a lease every so often when connected to a client. Halfway through the lease agreement, the client begins the renewal process. If the sever that originally granted the request is unavailable, the client will try again at a later date. If it cannot connect to the original server, then it will send a request to a backup server. Once it contacts the backup server, said server will renew the lease and update its client information. This can get tricky if the original server ever comes back into play. If a client can't get a hold of a backup server, it must start the address process all over again and rebind to a new server. This means it has to go through the DORA process all over again. Once it is set up, it will once again be able to connect to the servers, but all former connections will be lost.

☐ Security- The base protocol does not have any protection against attacks on its servers. These attacks can come in one of three ways.

- Unauthorized servers providing false information to its clients: Because there is no way to validate a server, rogue DHCPs can connect to a client and send them false information. This can serve as a DoS attack or a middle man to send information back to a hacker. This can allow a hacker to eavesdrop on everything going on in the server.

-Unauthorized clients gaining information on the servers: Because there is no way to authenticate clients, they can hack into a server with fake credentials, and gain access to all the information stored in the databases and have access to some personal information.

-Resource exhaustion attacks: Malicious users hack onto a server and use up all the IP addresses stored so no one can access the sever, leaving them with no connection. This is a cruel and selfish thing to do.

While DHCP does have some protocols for fixing these problems, they are not really reliable, and there have not been more means to fix them. So if you do look into hacking, finding solutions to these problems would be a good idea.

--NAT- Network Address Translation. This maps an address space into another by modifying network packets. It is extremely popular over the Ipv4 network where all the individual IP addresses are exhausted. Instead it maps one over different hosts.

NAT usually consists of private networks where it maps one address space to another space. The translation it uses frees state table resources, and prevents network exhaustion. This begins only when the communication is activated, rather than running constantly. This makes the process a little slower, but keeps the resources in check. Due to its popularity, NAT is now synonymous with IP masquerading.

The majority of Nats are from many private networks to one public resource. The router has a private address while being connected to a public address that was already assigned. The router tracks only the basic data, rather than every increment of data that passes through its system to avoid being bogged down. It is a good solution to the impending doom of Ipv4, and keeps it in play for a few more years. Eventually Ipv4 will phase out entirely. To keep this at bay NAT needs many modifications. This is a good thing to use your hacking skills on.

--Private vs Public IP

Private have an internal IP address. This is issued by the router itself, rather than an external entity. This gives your device a unique fingerprint for the network it is on. These are the ones set up on DHCP (Read above), and they never leave your network.

Public has an external IP address that is assigned by the internet provider. This is assigned to the router itself, which transmits the information to the towers. Just like Private never leaves its network, Public Ips never enter the network.

--Routers and switches- These are both devices that allow multiple consoles to connect to a network, however their functions are all different. A router is a device that connects multiple networks, while a switch connects multiple devices to one network.

There are other things you need to learn too, such as Mac Addressing, ARP subnetting and VLANs.

- Linux Skills- another skill you should learn is Linux. Most programs derive from some sort of Linux system. Linux gives you more options than windows. There are many tutorials online, and they are very easy to follow.

Linux is free to obtain, unlike most software for hacking, however some features still must be paid for. You can get more free features when purchasing online, however, so it is always cheaper to go that route. \

- Security Technology- You must know the ins and outs of security software, that way you know what you are up against. You need to learn about secure sockets layer, intrusion detection system, firewalls, and public key infrastructure. A beginner can take a tutorial course such as Security +

- Wireless Technology- Basic knowledge about wireless encryption algorithms is essential. You should learn about wpa, wpa2, and wep. Also understanding protocol for authentication and legal constraints for wireless connections always proves helpful. Learning about wireless technologies is essential when you want to become a hacker, because one of the best things to hack, to get the information you need, is the wireless connection itself. In fact, you can often get information from more than one device at a time when you hack the source of wireless information itself.

- Virtualization- you need to be well versed in at least one of the many virtualization. These allow you a safe area to practice hacking without legal implications, at least until you venture out to try your hand in the real world. A few to try are VirtualBox, and VMWare Workstation.

- Programming- (see more in the chapter labeled programming) This is essential for a hacker to know if he ever wants to be more than a script kiddie. There are several languages you should know, but at the very least, you should choose one programming language to learn. There are five languages that are important to learn if you want to become a master hacker.

  ☐ Ruby- This is an easy to learn language that is a great starter language for beginners, as it reads almost like the English language. It is fun as well as functional, and it is a very productive language. It became popular through a framework entitled Ruby on the Rails. This frame work was designed for user enjoyment, and has been used to create many popular websites, such as AirBnb, Hulu, Bloomberg, and Shopify. This language is generally used for most backend developments, and is intended to be enjoyable.

  ☐ Java- A portable language that is designed to be used on any platform or device, and is a standard for mobile apps and most video interactive sites. This makes it of utmost importance to learn. It is not the same as javascript as java is a programming language, and javascript is a scripting language.

  ☐ C++- This is one of the most popular and versatile languages out there. It is used for most programs and internet sites. It is also used in some newer developments. Most of the social sites, and video games you use and play have been created by using C++. This is one of the fastest, most powerful languages there is, and makes it the main language of many powerful hackers.

- Python- This is not a beginner language. This is a language you learn once you learn the others, and have mastered them quite well. This is the language that are used by big name companies, such as NASA, Yahoo, and Google. This is not a programming language, but in reality, it is a scripting language. This means that you can produce a lot of code in a very short amount of time. The most important thing to know about Python, is that it is not easy to learn, so don't get discouraged if it takes you awhile to get the hang of it.

- C- This is the influence of almost all other programming languages. While learning this can help you learn the others, it is the least popular among other hackers, as it requires long and super complex codes for even the simplest of tasks. This makes it undesirable, and nearly useless. However, the knowledge of it is still helpful when learning hacking.

While there is many arguments over which language you should learn first, in reality, it all depends on what kind of hacker you want to become. If you want to start out with an easier language, then Ruby would be a good start. If you want something more versatile, C++ would be what you are looking for. It all depends on your style. With some patience and hard work, you can master these skills, you can begin to learn other things once mastering languages, such as databases, and TCP/IP, and so on and so forth.

- TCP/ICP Traffic and Attacks- This is something you should learn as a hacker, as it will help you learn more about wireless networks. There are many different tools to use for this, such as wireshark and TCPdump.

Chapter 6: Hacking Tips:

This is the moment you have been waiting for, actual hacking tips! These tips will help you become a great hacker, and give you tips on how to avoid being caught. In the next chapter there will be a (fictional) story about what can happen if you do not take precautions, and end up getting caught. Be careful out there my hacker friends, as hacking is a risky business. Protect yourselves and your computers.

VPN

This stands for Virtual Private Network, and is essential to avoid being caught by law enforcement in your hacking endeavors. They create anonymity by using an encrypted connection to network that is not so secure. This will allow you to hide your IP address online. There are a lot sites you use to find VPN on.

- ZenMate VPN- With servers in twenty countries and one hundred and twenty eight bit encryption by AES, this service is a great one for a beginning hacker. You get a one month free trial, but then you unfortunately have to pay. At least you can get a feel for the program before you have to front some money.

- VyprVPN- While you only have three days to try this site out before paying, it is very versatile, and even has mobile apps. On the plus side, you don't have restrictions, or even data caps.

- ExpressVPN- for the major hacker. This site is coming out with a thirty day trial, allowing you to get a feel for its two hundred and fifty six bit encryption by AES. Even though it is powerful, it is easy to use and comes with a great customer support service team.

- PureVPN- This service is one of the most expansive with hundreds of servers in over forty one countries. While it is fast and does not allow anyone in a third party to track your usage, it does not come with a free trial, so you would have to pay before deciding if you like the product or not.

Those are just some of the sites that help you set up a VPN. I am sure that you can find some that are free online, but be warned, they may not be reliable. Hiding from the law can be an expensive business, so only the best should be used in this case. Spending twenty dollars a month is better than spending twenty years in jail.

More about VPN-

VPN is a private network that extends across a public one. It protects your identity as if you were directly connected to a personal network that hid your IP address from view. A VPN can provide a private, functional space for you to work with, but be careful, as some may sell your information rather than protect it. This could put you at risk for being spied upon by a cop. VPN has more uses than just hacking as well. Business owners can allow their employees to connect to the business intranet when away from the office, that way they can still telecommute even when they are ill. It can be used to securely connect different offices that are in different parts of the country, or even across the globe. You can use it to secure transmissions across the wireless board, protect your identity, and even get around some geographical restrictions on a website.

A VPN uses a point-to-point connection to become established. It uses dedicated encryption, and tunneling and traffic protocols. It can help create some of the benefits you would get from a wide access network, or WAN.

A VPN can be activated by either remote access, or port-to-port access. Remote allows employees to connect while outside the office, meanwhile port to port allows geographical connection.

VPNs have many security measures to protect their user's identity, and any information shared across these networks. As long as the VPN site is secure, and legitimate, it will be a good setup to use for hacking. No one can track your IP address, as it really does not exist within a virtual private network. It would be like you were not even there.

Password Cracking

This is a very Neanderthal method of hacking, for those types of hackers that only want into a social media site. This type of hacking is also known as Brute Force Hacking, as it literally uses the electronic version of what brute force is. You force your way into a system by finding out the password. To find out the password, you have to go through every possible option. Just like trying to break down a door with a log, this can take a long time. The length of time this may take, can be extremely long, depending on how long the password is. Even with a computer this is a slow process, and should only be used when you cannot find a back door. Otherwise you waste a lot of time, when you could have been in in five minutes or less. There are several sites that can help you with password cracking.

- Brutus- aptly named for brute force hacking, this wonderful tool is only available on Windows, but it is claimed to be the fastest tool available, and is able to be controlled remotely. As an added perk, it is also free. So if you are a Windows lover, this is the tool for you.

- John the Ripper- Obviously a play on the name Jack the Ripper, this tool is popular and free. It works on all types of systems no matter what platform they operate, and combines all sorts of brute force hacking packages in one convenient place. It also automatically detects special characters such as hyphens and dashes, and is customizable.

- WFUzz- This tool is a must try for beginners, and it combines many tools into one, even an SQL injector, and processor. It is web based, so you will need an internet connection to run it. But if you are trying to hack someone's personal sites, more than likely you are already on the internet.

- THC Hydra- also another really fast cracking tool that is great for beginners. It is flexible, and works on pretty much all of the operating systems there are. It also allows you to add new modules easily.

More about password cracking

Password cracking is the act of retrieving a password through the data that has been transmitted and stored on the computer. The most common approach is the brute force technique where you guess the password repeatedly and check it across the network data that has been stored. This is not only used to gain unlawful access, but also to try to get into a site that you forgot your password to when you don't have administrator privileges. It is also used to gain access to a file that has been permitted access too, yet it is still restricted.

Most people are predictable, they will chose a password that is easy for them to remember, therefor it is also easy to guess, if you know the person well enough, but on the rare occasion that you do not know the person, or they do not chose an easy to guess password. A lot of people also do not follow the standards of changing the password once a month. They also do not use the proper mix of uppercase, lowercase, and special characters, as they do not want to risk forgetting their password.

There are many types of software out there that will teach you how to crack passwords, some of them are noted above, and will even help you. There are several others online, and most of them are free. But again always scan your download before usage, to avoid viruses.

Shutting Down Computers Remotely

You have the power to shut down someone else's computer from the comfort of your own home. You can shut down nearly anyone on the globe this way. It is a power that should not be used on a whim. This is a power that can get you in a heap of trouble or be your best friend. If the computer is in your network, you only need to know its name. There are a few simple steps you have to follow to do so.

1. Pull up the search bar

2. Type cmd. This will open the command center

Optional. You can type in "color a" to bring up a list of hacker colors. Generally black or green

3. Type "net view"

4. Hit enter. This will show you all the computers on your network.

5. Type shut down.

6. Fill out all the options in the box. It will ask you a few questions. Just answer them with random answers and chose if you want to display a warning message, and for how long.

A computer shutdown for a computer that is not on your network is a little trickier. This involves knowing the computers IP address. To practice this, you may want to begin on your own computer, so that you don't get into any trouble. You can go to www.whatismip.com. To practice this on your own computer, follow the same steps that you would for a computer in your own network, except type in the IP address instead of the computer name.

More about shutting down computers remotely

Shutting down computers remotely is a risky business if you do not own them. You can easily get caught, and the penalty is severe, as it is considered a form of vandalism. You are rendering an object that is not yours inoperable, and therefore, you have electronically broken someone else's property.

If you are granted permission to shut down computers remotely, you can do so freely. As long as you have permission from someone in the right places. If you are getting permission from a friend, its better not to. However, if you are getting permission from the federal government, then you can safely go ahead. Show off your skills, and shut that computer down.

Practicing Command Prompts

As the administrator with full privileges on you r computer, you can use command prompts to do whatever you please on your computer. This can help you practice hacking in a legal manner. As long as you are using your own personal computer, you can ethically practice using the CMD prompts.

You can add or delete members on your computer, and you can add or take away administrator privileges. You can use a test account to try this out without messing with any of your personal files.

To try this out use the following steps

1. Open the command prompt

2. Type "net user test/add" (you can replace test with whatever word you need)

3. Hit enter

4. Go into the control center to ensure this worked

5. Open command prompt

7. Type "net local group administrators test/add"

8. Hit enter. This should give admin privileges to your test dummy account.

Optional- if you want to get into this account simply type in net user, and you don't need a password to access these accounts.

9. Open command prompt

10. Type "net user test/delete"

11. Hit enter. This will delete the test dummy account

Among these command prompts, there are a few more that it is always a good idea to know. Becoming familiar with these is always a good idea, as you will become a better hacker. And if your dream is to become a master, laziness, is not an endeavor you want to foresee. The prompts you should know are:

- Tracet- This allows a person to track the network movements that a packet travels as it enters the wireless stream from your computer to its destination port. It also tracks the length that each jump will take, and can trace up to thirty jumps at one time. Type "tracet-n (number you want to track) into command prompt to specify the number you want to track.

- Ping Host- This verifies making contact with a machine's host. This commands the internet control message protocol or ICMP for short. There are ping packets that will tell you how long it takes a machine to respond. The machine may not respond at all. To do so do as follows.

1. Type "ping"

2. Hit space

3. Type the IP address.

4. Hit enter

-Optional you can send multiple ping packets by typing "ping-n (number of packets you wish to send)

- IP configuring- This is the command you use to display the host's active network. You do this by typing "ipconfig/all" you can also use "ipcinfig/renew" to renew your IP address. You can also use it to deactivate networks as well.

- Netstat- This will tell you the status of a network. It also establishes connections using remote devices. Type 'netstat-a' to check connections and listing ports. Type 'netstat-n' to see port numbers and addresses portrayed in numeric form. 'netstat-e' to check Ethernet stats. There are also more options to check things and combine them as well. Fiddle around with it to figure out what works and what doesn't.

- Route Print- This is used to delete or set up static routes. You can display route lists, add and delete routes. There are many other options this has as well. Practicing will allow you to get accustomed with this process.

Thinking Like a Hacker

You have to think like a hacker to be a hacker. If you don't have the mindset, then you will not be able to be a successful hacker, and will not make it very far. Also, thinking like a hacker will help protect you from being discovered, or being struck with viruses from other hackers. There are a few things you should follow when thinking like a hacker.

1. Identify the domain name of potential exploits. This requires you to gather all the information you can, to make an electronic footprint. Learn everything you can about a company, and record all their information. IP addresses, domain names, phone numbers, subsidiaries, security systems, and access points. Once you have all of this information, you can then begin your hack, based on the Intel you have gathered.

2. Look for a back door. This is when a security system is weak in places, or compromised from a company buyout. These back doors will help you find you way in unseen, rather than having to worry about being detected by a firewall.

3. Once you have gained all the necessary information, begin an attack known as a Trojan horse. This will allow you to sneak in on the back of a desirable item, and infect their systems with viruses and malware.

It is important to think like a hacker before you start hacking, as it will make you feel more professional. The more professional you feel, the better you learn, because you apply yourself more. It is important to apply yourself, because hacking is an ever changing business that you have to stay ahead of. If you can stay ahead of the game, you will be a success. Follow these tips, and you will be a successful hacker.

Conclusion

Thank you for buying this book. I hope you enjoyed the information that is contained in these pages, and enjoyed the journey through the steps it takes to begin hacking. In this book we discovered new things about hacking, and how to go about learning new things to become the best hacker you can be. If you follow this book, and keep it with you as a guide on your journey, and you will be a success. I wish you the best of luck, and happy hacking!

www.ingramcontent.com/pod-product-compliance
Lightning Source LLC
Chambersburg PA
CBHW071030050326
40689CB00014B/3589